To _____

Thank you for purchasing my book. May the Lord bless you.

_____

George C. Duke

Date _____

JUST A COP
By George Duke

INDEX

About

FOREWORD

Try to imagine what might happen if there were no policemen around. And then try to think of ways to make their job rewarding. Show them respect offer them a smile and a kind word. Remember there can be Physical Injuries and sometimes Physical death can occur while one is serving as a law Enforcement Officer. One never knows when it can or will occur, if he did then it might be possible to avoid it. So when one chooses this arena he or she must expect danger or death to be lurking in the shadow of time. From the time that he reports for duty until the time his shift ends a Policeman must stay alert and on guard as he never knows when this could be the very moment or day he faces a dangerous situation where he might be injured or even die. "A policeman is many things. He's a son, a brother, a father, an uncle, and sometimes a grandfather. He is a protector in the time of need and a comforter in time of sorrow. Sometimes his job calls for him to be a diplomat, a psychologist, a lawyer, a friend, and an inspiration. He suffers from an overdose of publicity about brutality and dishonesty along with notoriety produced by unfounded charges. Too often acts of heroism go unnoticed and the truth is buried under all the criticism. The fact is that less than one-half of one per cent of our policemen ever discredits their uniform. That's a better average than you'll find among clergymen."" A policeman is an ordinary guy who is called upon for extraordinary bravery--for us! As you read this book you might note some of the near-death experiences that I faced in the physical realm. Most of them occurred when I least expected it. It happened so quickly and was over before I even realized I was in danger. Also there were comical times that when I remember them they still cause me to laugh.

You will find

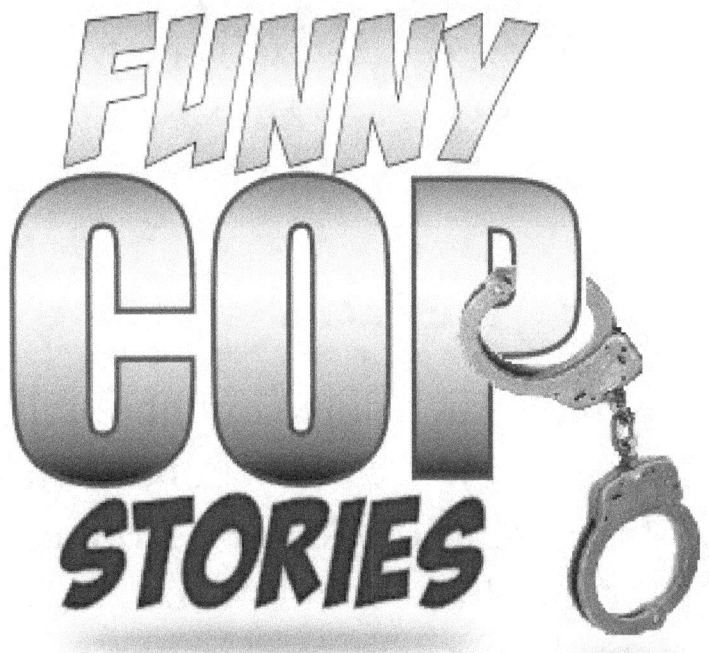

I rear-ended a car this morning.
So, there we were alongside the road and
slowly the other driver got out of his car.
You know how sometimes you just get
soooo stressed and little things just seem
funny?
Yeah, well I couldn't believe it.... he was a
DWARF!!!
He stormed over to my car, looked up at me,
and shouted, 'I AM NOT HAPPY!!!'
So, I looked down at him and said, 'Well,
then which one are you?'

And that's how the fight started...

Me Factor

After driving a truck since my honorable discharge from the U.S. Air Force I chose to accept the offer to become a Police Officer for the Pensacola Police department. From the time I began my duties as a peace officer till I left the force so many things happened in my life. As I think of many of these events I realize how Gods hand had been upon my life. After being accepted into the Pensacola Police Department I started my training. After my training, I started my first day as a Police Officer badge # 40. My heart was beating fast as I took over the driver position in the 1955 Ford police cruiser for the first time. On my first day of duty after the two weeks of classroom and pistol range classes I am placed in a car with the Shift Captain who instructed me to do the driving. "Where would you like me to go, Sir? I asked him?" "Just drive and I will let you know as we tour the area the captain said." I knew that he could feel my trembling as I spoke because it showed in my voice.

While driving around the Pensacola area we were traveling west on Cervantes street when the call came in. Captain, what's your 10-20? Cervantes and Baylen he replied. Captain, there's a 10-33 at Palafox and Maxwell. 10-4 the Captain replied. The captain looked at me ok let's go. With a giant lump swelling up in my throat I slowly reached down and turned the red light and siren on. Ok here's my chance to show him what I am made of entered into my mind as I stomped down on the accelerator making the turn from Cervantes street onto Palafox street as fast as I could and lo and behold in front of me just 3 blocks I saw the red light at the intersection! Yes, I am a Policeman with an emergency and no red light was going to slow me down, with siren screaming and red light flashing I blasted through that light at 60 mph. The Captain slowly looked over at me and said," Duke we slow down at red lights and make sure the intersection is clear before we go through it." If it had been possible at that moment I would have hung my head down in shame but I kept my eyes on the road and said: "Yes Sir."

Arriving at the scene of the accident I noted a woman that had been rear-ended by another driver who was screaming out in agony. I ran up to her and asked her if I needed to call an ambulance? Moaning she looked at me and in a weak voice said noooo, I should be able to get out of the car, just give me a moment. I turned around to the other driver and asked him to produce his driver's license and Insurance. He pulled out his driver's license and handed it to me and stated I do not have insurance! Suddenly the Lady in the rear-ended vehicle leaped out of her car screaming, "You don't have insurance? " The sudden knowledge of his having no insurance healed her completely.

After calling for a wrecker, investigating the accident, clearing the intersection, and issuing my first ticket I got back into the patrol car and left the scene. On arrival back at police headquarters, the Captain informed me that he was placing me with another officer for the rest of my shift. Well now I am no longer driving and the officer he has twinned me with is a man that speaks very little and when he does he speaks very slowly. We were together less than an hour when we receive a call, "Disturbance at a West sidebar." We rapidly make our way over to the bar and I leaped out of the car and rush inside. The bartender comes over and speaks to us about a man who is drunk and abusive. I go over to the white male who he has pointed out and grab him by his arm pulling him toward the door. He begins to resist me and I grab him in a hold and my partner helps me get him outside. We handcuff the prisoner and place him in the back of the squad car and take him to the jail to be booked.

After we had completed booking the prisoner in, we went back to the patrol car and as we were pulling out of the station my partner looked over at me and said slowly with a drawl, "Duke if you would like me to, I could tell you how to avoid a lot of resisting arrests? " My reply was yes please tell me and slowly he began to inform me what I had done wrong and what I needed to do to prevent most resisting arrests. "Duke, when you make an arrest, do not grab a person, as most people do not like for someone to manhandle them even if it is a policeman. Just go up to them and gently touch them on the shoulder and tell them they are under arrest and would they come with you? Normally 90% will come with you without resisting." I looked at him and let him know I really appreciated his advice.

I used that advice for the rest of my time on the Police Force and found that he was 100% accurate. In all of the future arrests that I made I only had two that resisted. After riding with a partner for a week and learning the routine my training time for being in a patrol car came to an end, then I found out what it was like to walk a beat. For the next week, I was placed on foot patrol with a partner to break me in and show me the area and to introduce me to businessmen and women in the areas where foot patrols were used. After the week was over I suddenly found myself walking a beat solo. Most of the time a Rookie would find himself walking the beat in Brownsville which is a small suburb on the west side of Pensacola. It has quite a lot of businesses on the main street. As it was quite a distance from the central business area, so it was not considered a favorite beat with many of the Policemen. Let me share some short stories of incidents that I was involved in during my tenure as a Cop.

The police came to my house earlier & said my dog had chased someone on a bike. I said, you must be joking officer, my dog hasn't got a bike.

when police received the calls.

MOUNTAIN VIEW

FRIDAY

Wal-Mart: Police receive a report of a newborn infant found in a trash can. Upon investigation, officers discover it was only a burrito.

ATHERTON

THURSDAY

JUST A COP

Really my life as a Cop was not just having donuts and coffee as some might imagine.

I would like to give you an as accurate to the best of my knowledge undeniable proof of my actions while serving as some of you would call, "A Cop" and considering your desires as indispensable orders for the truth, the whole truth, and nothing but the truth. Ungracious then as the task may be, I shall try to recall some of the events and even some near death experiences of those dangerous stages of my police life, out of which I emerged, at length, to the enjoyment of every blessing in the power of love, health and fortune. There were many awesome events that occurred during my service on the Pensacola Police Department. It was during my tenure as a cop that many sit ins and demonstrations at the various department stores occurred in which I had to make many arrests. Some of the major stores were the Woolworth Store and Kress's, as well as some drug stores. It was during the time of my service that I was shocked by the news of the murder of President Robert Kennedy in which my

Brother Robert Duke had written about Jeanne Dixons prophesy on his death.

The Sit In Years

One of the first things that you learn that is your real duty while serving on the Police Force is that you must enforce the law that you agree with as well as the law you may disagree with.

Your duty is not to self but to all of the people no matter whom or what they might be. The sit ins occurred because of segregation between black and white people and was very prevalent at the time that I joined the Pensacola Police Department. I had not been on the force very long before we begin to have the sit in demonstrations in the department stores that had restaurants such as

Woolworths. What would happen doing these demonstrations would be that as segregated white people were sitting at the counter, eating or drinking coffee or soft drinks suddenly black people would walk in and sit at the counter with them?

Most of the white people would leave or ignore the situation but there would eventually be someone that opposed their being there. So how would a Cop handle the situation? Let me answer this by saying that before we were assigned duty in the department store we all had to meet together with the Chief of Police who instructed us on how to handle any violence that might occur. Much of the time when I had this duty there would always be someone there to start trouble. So the major solution for the Police Officer was to arrest both of the people involved in the affray and then allow the Judge in the court hearing to decide the guilt or innocence of the individuals and this was a solution that I agreed with. I remember my brother who was a Newspaper reporter attending one of the demonstrations when an arrest had to be made. Not only were the demonstrators in the stores but they also were doing sit ins on the buses.

During my years of having to deal with these sit ins I only had one call to handle an affray on the city bus as normally the bus driver would ask both parties involved to get off the bus. It was only when they refused that the bus driver would call for the Police to handle the situation. I remember being called on that one occasion that I mentioned and arriving found that a while male and a black male were almost ready to fist fight. What did not help the situation was that their girlfriends and others on the bus was what we use to call egging them on hoping that they would be able to see a real fight. Well I arrested both and took them to the police station to be booked.

spected at a U.S. Department of Agriculture facility on Witmer Road.

The truck driver told police they weren't "dealing with normal cows." They made their escape after pushing a release button.

"He said that they were smart cows, and they must have been planning this for a while," Suitor said.

The two cows remained on the lam late Wednesday night.

YES OFFICER, I DID SEE THE "SPEED LIMIT" SIGN, I JUST DIDN'T SEE YOU.

He was just sleeping

It was on a Sunday night after midnight that I suddenly came upon a house that was on fire. When I first saw the flames I could hardly believe what I was seeing. The winds were blowing toward the west which held back the progression of the fire and as you watched it appeared to be just burning the front room and going no further. Since the fire appeared to have been burning for quite awhile one would have expected for anyone inside to have already evacuated. I picked up my radio and called the fire department and gave them the location. After reporting the fire

I jumped out and began to see if I could locate anyone that had left the building. There was no one anywhere that had been inside. All of a sudden a lady ran up and informed me that she knew the male that lived there and suspected that he might have started the fire accidentally because he had been drunk that night and she had seen him stagger into the front door smoking. After receiving her report that there might be someone inside I ran around to the back door and climbed up the stairs and went inside. As I entered the rear of the house I began to call out,"Is there anyone inside? Is there anyone inside?" It was so filled with smoke that I only made it about 10 feet inside before I was overcome. I staggered back outside and began to try to figure out a way to get inside to the front of the home. Another police officer arrived and told me to get down on the floor and crawl toward the front of the house. He joined with me and we finally got to the front and there was a bed where a man was laying near it on the floor. We grabbed him and kept down on the floor slowly pulling him to the back door. As we got near the door a couple of firemen arrived with breathing gear and helped us outside. The fire department treated the man until an ambulance arrived and took him to the hospital. Later I found out that after extinguishing the fire that the fire had started by a cigarette igniting the mattress in the front room where we had located the man laying on the floor. The next day during the day light hours I traveled back to look at the home. What had really saved that man's life was the wind causing the fire to hold from spreading and a cop that just happened to be patrolling in the area. Many miraculous things are performed by cops just in the line of duty. Truly God loves Cops; maybe that is why the world sometimes despises them.

THE LITTLE GREEN MEN

It was on a Sunday night that I had to work as the dispatcher as our regular dispatcher was off. I had been on duty for a few hours and it appeared to be a slow night. All of a sudden the telephone rang and when I answered the call, Pensacola Police Department Officer Duke can I help you. The voice on the line was a woman with a heavy British accent asking me to send the police, send the police. I asked her to calm down and give the address and why she needed the Police. Officer Duke there is three little green men sitting on my bed. Three green men I asked. She said yes. I asked what are they doing? They are pointing at me and laughing she replied. Where did they come from was my next question? They came out of the television set and ran into my bedroom. By this time I knew I had a case on my hands. Now how do I deal with it? Ok are they still in the bedroom I asked. Yes and they just keep staring at me and making fun. All right now here is what I want you to do. Go in the bedroom and order them to leave. I have already done that several times Officer Duke. They will not leave. By this time I realized I had a REAL case on my hands. So I decided to become one also. Ok now go in there and say Ookie bookie wookie and they will disappear. Pardon me she said. Go in there and say ookie bookie wookie and they will go. Will you wait for me to do it? Oh yes I will wait. Then I heard her lay the telephone down and walk into the other room and utter the words I had told her to say. When she returned she said I said ookie lookie wookie but they did not go away. I asked her what were the exact words that you said. Ookie lookie wookie she answered. I said well there is your problem, I said Ookie bookie wookie not ookie lookie wookie. So they are still there I asked and she replied Yes. Ok I will have Officer Stevens to come out and get rid of them. She thanked me and hung up. On the Radio I called for car 25 and when they answered I asked them to respond to the address. What's the problem Stevens asked. Signal 25 (Crazy Person) seeing little green men that came out from behind the TV set. 10-4 he replied on my way.

After dispatching the Police car to her address another call came in from another woman that asked me to send a policeman to South Palafox Street. I asked her what she needed a Policeman for and she said I just need one so send him now. I could tell that she was drunk and more than likely would be arrested if I sent an officer out. I think a good thing for you to do since you appear to be intoxicated is to go home. No I want you to send me a Cop. I gotta have a Cop I gotta have a Cop Send him now

Why I asked again? Ok if you have to know because I need a Man!

Finally I sent her a man and she got free room and board for the night but she got no man except the one that arrested her and placed her in jail for being drunk and disorderly!

Later that night when the shift had ended I asked Don what happened when he went out to the house. His reply was I went inside and she said they had ran under the bed when I entered the house. So I went into the bedroom and pulled up the sheet bent over and shouted under the bed GET OUT OF HERE! Then I went over to her and said they were gone then I instructed her to call me Don Stevens if they come back. Then I asked Don did he see anything under the bed when he looked? He laughed and said Nope!

The Car Thief

The clock had already struck the 11:00 hour on Saturday night when the paddy wagon dropped me off on the corner of Palafox and Gregory Street to walk beat 5 and 6. As it drove off and faded into the distance I looked around and suddenly, I spotted a man in the rear of the Hill-Kelly used car lot walking around. As I kept a watch on him I began to wonder, "Why would someone this late in the night be looking at cars," Moving over into the shadows I continued to keep my eyes on him to see what he was doing and if I could identify him? Was he on our wanted list? Suddenly as he turned his face toward me and then I realized that here was a man that was wanted for Auto theft and embezzlement. Had he seen me and moved to the back of the car lot to avoid being captured or was he looking for another vehicle to heist? All kind of thoughts raced through my mind as I approached him, then suddenly when he spotted me walking toward him, I could tell he did not know what to do, and as he turned toward me I recognized him as a person I knew very well by the name of Munsey Dees. Quickly I walked up to him, and said, you are under arrest! Turn around and place your hands behind your back, I commanded. He turned and I quickly placed the handcuffs on his wrists. After handcuffing him we walked back to the corner where a call box was located and I called for a squad car to come and pick him up. Rolling up to the corner in a black and white patrol car, the two officers jumped out and I informed them that I had captured him in the car lot and that he was wanted for car theft. I also let them know that there was a one hundred dollar reward for his arrest. Who is he, they asked? Munsey Dees I replied. Placing him in the back of the patrol car they looked at me and said good work and drove away to book him at the Police Station. Munsey was a white male that had worked as a salesman at Ocean City Auto Sales in Fort Walton Beach, Florida. He became fed up with his job and decided to take the cash and a car and leave. I had not been on the Pensacola Police force long when a man who ran the car lot reported the theft. At the time I did not know that Munsey was a nephew of the car lot owner when he instructed me to let other Policemen know he would give a $100 reward to anyone capturing Munsey. When I informed him that I had captured Munsey he was thrilled but when he told his brother, his brother was furious, not with Munsey but with his brother in law and me. Well, guess if I ever received my $100.00? This loss made me realize that rewards need to be made officially to the department.

Police: where do you live?
Me: with my parents
Police: where does your parents live?
Me: with me
Police: where do you all live ?
Me: together
Police: Where is your house?
Me: Next to my neighbors house.
Police: Where is your neighbors house?
Me: If I tell you, you won't believe me.
Police: Tell me.
Me: Next to my house.

"He was about five ten, wearing a camo shirt
and one of those funny Elmer Fudd type hats.
He pointed the gun right at me!"

THE PENNY ANTE BOYS

As I was cruising down Palafox street after passing the gas station I slowed down as I approached the Maxwell street crossing in order to look over at the launderette located about a half block to the west of Palafox. Making a quick glance toward the building I noticed out of the corner of my eye a shadow on the inside of the building. I continued to drive south and a few blocks down I made a u-turn and proceeded to travel back to the laundry mat. I drove slowly pass the building noting that the door was partially open. I did not see anyone inside and continued on west on Maxwell to where it made a left curve. As I drove around the curve I noticed a car parked on the side of the darkened street. I looked at the car to see if I could see anyone inside but it appeared to be empty and the windows were all raised. After passing the car I made another u-turn and turned off my headlights and approached the Laundry mat again. I turned off my engine about 500 feet from the building and I allowed my cruiser to coast up to where I could look inside the building. Yes there they were. Three young men were busy attempting to break open the coin boxes on the machines. I reached for the mike for my radio and attempted to call for back-up. The radio was filled with chatter and I tried to break in but to no avail. After several failed attempts I noted that suddenly the men inside had spotted my car and was about to attempt to get away. I leaped out of the car and ran towards them telling them to halt. They ran towards me and two of them began to wrestle with me as the third man ran away. As we wrestled I was unable to get to my black jack or weapon as they had a hold on my arms. Out of the corner of my eyes I spotted the gas station attendant looking my way and I called out for him to call for back-up. When I called out for help suddenly two of the men grabbed me and began to wrestle with me while the third man stood in the back ground. Overpowering me they eventually tossed me to the ground and ran away. As I rose up off the ground and watched them disappear in opposite directions I took off running after the one that appeared to be the slowest. There is an old saying on the Police force better one in hand than three in the bush. I finally captured him and placed my handcuffs on him and placed him in the back seat of the patrol car which had a mesh metal enclosed back seat and doors that could not be opened from the inside. I got in and grabbed my radio again requesting back-up and soon there were other patrol cars on the scene. We begin to search the area and attempt to locate the other two men that had escaped. After searching for a while I stopped in at the gas station and asked the attendant why he had not called in for help for me. He looked at me with shock and said that he could not hear what I had said. He also stated that since he could not distinguish that I was a Policeman nor did he see my car he thought that it was just someone cutting up in front of the laundry. As I still had my prisoner in the car I eventually made another cruise around the area and as I did I noted that the car that I had seen on the curve was still parked just off the roadway. I took the prisoner in and booked him then traveled back to the scene. The car was still there. I then drove pass the car just pass the curve and turned around where I could see the car from a distance. I did not have to wait very long before I saw two figures in the woods across the street from the car look both ways before crossing the street. As soon as I saw them I called for back-up which came this time very quickly and as they opened the door I sped up to their car blocking it. I pulled my weapon and ordered them to lean against the car. I made a search and then cuffed them and placed them into the cruiser in the back seat. The very first thing that they did was to apologize and ask me where their partner was. I informed them that he was located at the city jail where they would be in a short time. As I drove in to the Police station I was very happy that I had been able to arrest all three and that all I suffered was falling down when they shoved me and ran.

Later after booking them and placing them in a jail cell I asked the radio dispatcher the reason I was unable to get help when I had called in. He stated that when I called it mixed with another cars call also which was involved in a high speed chase. Since my message was garbled he was not able to know who it was that had called nor was he able to decipher the location.

■ 4:21 p.m. — A report was taken about the theft of a cell phone from Commerce Way.

■ 5:00 p.m. — Police were called to Market Square for a report about a "suspicious coin." Investigating officer reported it was a quarter.

■ 5:45 p.m. — A Greenleaf Avenue caller reported someone was living under a ramp where

SPEEDY GONZALEZ

As I left the police station that night I drove back up to where I had been patrolling when I came across the penny ante burglars which had now been booked and jailed. As I was traveling along Palafox Street suddenly an automobile flashed out of nowhere and passed me at a high rate of speed. When he realized he had passed a police car he began to speed up even more. I immediately turned on my red lights and begin to pursue him. He then began to make erratic turns trying to shake me but when I turned on my siren and drew nearer to his vehicle he finally decided to pull over. As I was a little wary of what and why he had been speeding I took precautions as I got out of my car and approached him. He was a young white male and as soon as I came along the side of his window he began to apologize and tell me a story of why he was traveling so fast. Well his story was so interesting and heart touching that I finally let him go with a verbal warning. He looked at me and was so happy when he realized I was not going to arrest him or give him a ticket. As I traveled back to the cruiser I heard the radio calling my car number. I grabbed the mike and answered and was told that there was a prowler call at a residential area on my beat. I told them I was on the way. I traveled to a home on East strong street and knocked on the door of the address that was given. The lady of the house answered the door and in a shaky voice began to relate to me how a man knocked on her door. When she answered the door there stood a male all dressed up as a female. I guess this was the first time I had heard about a transgender which term we did not use in that day and time. Well she gave me the description of the person and I told her not to worry that I would walk around the area and see if I could locate this person. As I left her home I began looking around and had walked about a total of four to five blocks. I turned around and headed back towards her house to let her know that I had not seen anyone matching her prowler. As I neared her home there in front of me was a woman well I thought it was a woman walking toward me. I looked at her/him and when I said hello and called out have you seen any strangers in the area she instantly turned around and ran. I took off in pursuit and in those days I was able to run fairly well. I grabbed her and stopped her and her wig fell off and he surrendered. I placed him under arrest for disturbing the peace and questioned him about what he was doing in the area and how did he get there. He then confessed to what he had done and informed me that he had a car around the corner. I traveled to where he said his vehicle was located and found it where he had said it was located. I began to do a search of the car and noted that it was filled with female attire. Also I located a suitcase that was full of ladies under garments. After booking him at the jail I then went back to policing my area. On the way I stopped by and let the lady know that I had caught and booked her prowler. She was very happy and said I feel more secure and at peace now. Well as I left the area where she lived I spotted a car speeding and took off in pursuit. When I finally got him stopped guess who it was? Yes it was speedy again. Well he again began to talk and before I knew it I was letting him go again without issuing him a ticket. As he drove away I asked myself Duke what's wrong with you letting him go twice. After all the excitement of the night I decided to drive over to Krispy Kreme donut shop and have a cup of coffee and a donut. Krispy Kreme had a great coffee area and normally you would always find a fellow officer either on duty or off duty there. The great thing about being a Cop was you always had close fellowship and friendship with the fellow officers on the force. Each time I would go into the coffee shop there was always a smiling friendly face and a warm greeting. After I had my coffee I went back on patrol duty driving around keeping an eye out for prowlers or any thing suspicious. As I drove along Ninth Avenue all of a sudden a car shot through a four way stop without stopping. Instantly I chased him down with my red light flashing and my siren screaming. He pulled over and when I approached his car I am sure you can guess who it was? Yes I had captured speedy Gonzalez again for the third time. As I neared the car window and saw who it was I looked at him and said well you are not going to talk me out of a ticket this time. Speedy looked at me and said Duke I am not even going to try. I wrote him a ticket and that was the last time I saw Speedy again.

The Saga of the Missing Eyebrow

Cruising down the river I was singing as I drove around my designated area of Pensacola while on one man squad car patrol one weekend. The day had gone well and actually it had been a little boring because the calls were few. As I begin to think about what I would do after my duty was ended suddenly a call came over the radio calling my car number. Car 19, car 19 go to Cervantes and L Street and investigate a disturbance. We have a report there is an accident at that location that may have injuries. I switched on my siren and turned around and headed in the direction given. Soon I was arriving on the scene and seconds later I was backed up by the duty sergeant. As I ran to the vehicle and looked inside I saw a woman laying there injured. I was surprised that the vehicle did not appear to be damaged.

So since there was no danger of it catching on fire I checked her over as much as possible. The only real injury I saw was bruises on her face. Then as I looked closer I noticed that over one of her eyes there was no eyebrow and blood was coming from the wound. I decided to wait for the ambulance to come before moving her but then she came to and began to scream and hold her hands over her eye. When she had regained consciousness she began to talk to me and told me that she had come to check on her husband. She thought he was inside the house nearby. The girl that lived there chased her away from the door and they became involved in an argument that resulted in a fight. Suddenly as she wrestled with the girl she was struck with a head butt and then the girl bit her over the eye. Staggering to the car she made it inside but must have passed out. As she felt her eye again she suddenly realized that her eyebrow was missing. At that time the ambulance arrived and the medical team ran over to the car and began to treat her wounds. They then loaded her up in the ambulance and drove away. After the ambulance had departed I continued the investigation by locating the girl that she had been involved in the ruckus with. After listening to her side of the story I decided to arrest her and allow the Judge to decide who was responsible. After completing the investigation and booking the girl I found that my shift had ended. I then turned in my car and entered the squad room to finish my report. While sitting there ready to complete my report the telephone rang. I answered it and I was surprised. The nurse at the hospital had called me to find out if I had found the lady's missing eyebrow. I assured her that I had not. She then asked me to go back and see if I could find it because they needed it to sew back on. I drove back out to the scene and looked around and then called the nurse and related to her that my search was negative. I could not locate the eyebrow.

THE HAPPY SAILORS

Sometimes you have to write about something you knew about for many years but you really did not know all there was to know. That may not make a lot of sense but maybe before I finish this story you will understand what I really meant. I really should have titled this The Dumb Cop. I was on the midnight shift walking beat four, five and six. As I strolled up the main street downtown around 1:00 am I heard a lot of loud noise and commotion coming from the western side of town. As there are no night clubs or bars open this late in the night I had to go check out what was making or causing the uproar. As I crossed the street suddenly I spotted a group of men singing and talking in very loud voices walking toward me. When they saw me they suddenly stopped their singing and quietened down. I walked up to them and found that they had been drinking but was not drunk just boisterous. I asked them what they were doing and one of the men apparently the leader said that they were coming from a party and was on their way to catch a bus back to the base. I asked them for their I.D. and they all pulled out their wallets and handed me their Navy I.D. I then told them to be a little quieter as they were being too loud and I did not want to have to arrest them for disturbing the peace. They seemed happy that I was not going to arrest them and the leader said say before we go back to base lets go get some coffee. As they walked away I noted that some of them had a strut in their walk that was like a woman but it was only a thought that soon vanished from my mind. Later that night I met up on the corner of my beat with a fellow officer by the name of Mandel who was walking beat one through three. The very first thing that he asked me was say did you see those gay Yankee sailors headed down to Trader Johns? I laughed and said yes I had stopped them for making two much noise and warned them about the noise. When they left me they had said they were headed to a coffee shop. Well they did not make it to the coffee shop. We had to arrest them down at Trader Johns for disturbing the peace. He then looked at me and said you knew they were gay didn't you? You should have known just by the way that they walked.

Many months later Mandel and I were working in a two man squad car on the East side of town. It was around midnight and we decided to check out a dirt road that ran along beside the railroad track just off of Gregory Street that many times was used as a lover's lane. As we drove along the road we noticed parked on the side was a beige station wagon. As we neared the vehicle I thought there was some movement and Mandel turned on the spotlight and shone it into the vehicle but it appeared to be empty. We continued on down the road a few blocks then made a u-turn and turned off our lights and slowly drove back to the station wagon. We grabbed our flashlights and quickly ran over to the rear and shone our light inside. Lo and behold there were two of the navy sailors pretending to be asleep in the vehicle. Mandel ordered them to get dressed and after they were dressed we placed them into the squad car and drove them to the Police station. Later after booking them for vagrancy Mandel explained what I had really seen was happy sailors. They must have had too much to drink I responded. Mandel gave me a funny look and smiled. Years later I would come to understand what that look meant. After picking them up they must have been transferred because we never saw them again.

Beats a Bicycle

Police checked the area and found an open door in the back of the building. An officer went inside and called out, "Marco."

The man's name was not Marco, detective Tim Dohr said. Instead, "the officer was trying to inject some humor into the situation."

Police found the suspect after he responded, "Polo."

The restaurant manager

THREE BLIND MISE?

Mice are small little creatures that can run around very fast and wriggle themselves out of difficult situations but then there comes along someone that either outruns them or traps them. Many times when they are caught they still can wriggle out of that trap. There is a very well known poem that is called, three blind mice written originally by Beatrice Potter that goes like this: Three blind mice! See how they run! They all ran after the farmer's wife, who cut off their tails with a carving knife.

Did you ever see such a thing in your life as three blind mice?

No and I never have seen young kids that could run around and get into so much trouble and when you finally catch them they still try to wriggle out of your trap. It was on the three to eleven shift one Saturday that the Captain instructed us to be on the look out for some kids that were doing a lot of thefts. He was not able to give any possible suspects to be on the look out for other than they had to be young because of the type of thefts they were involved in. After our briefing I walked out to my squad car and drove out of the rear driveway of the police station and jail. The rear entrance had a large field that you crossed then a few blocks further you began to get into the Aragon court housing area. As I entered the street to Aragon Court I noticed two kids riding away from the area on nice shiny bicycles. As I observed the kids I thought now where would a kid like that get such an expensive bike. He was coming from Aragon court and the people that lived there were in government low rental housing because of their income. I decided to check them out so I made my way toward them. When they spotted me coming their way one of them suddenly took off in another direction. I then took off after the one that was the nearest to me. So I pulled up in front of him and parked the squad car in such a way that he had to stop. Departing the car I walked over and began to question him about the bike he was riding. Is this your bike I asked? He assured me it was. Where did you get it? My parents got it for my birthday he replied. This lad was quick and answered all my interrogative questions in a reasonable manner but there was something about him that just was not right. He was nervous and would not look me in the eyes. All of a sudden I noticed him looking across the field. When I looked around to see what he was staring at there on the other side of the field was the other boy walking across the field toward us without the bicycle that I had seen him riding earlier. I ran over to where he was and quickly asked him where did you leave that stolen bike? Apparently he thought that the other boy had squealed on him and quickly replied in a crying manner Mister I left it over there pointing to the other side of the field. I took both boys into custody and when I questioned them further was able to discover where and when they had stolen the bicycles. They also related that they had stolen bikes before and either sold them to pals or anyone they could that would pay for them. I took them in to the Police station and booked them. The next day when I arrived for work I heard voices calling out from one of the cells above and looked up and there hanging on to the jail bars that they had climbed to look outside they called my name out. I looked up and smiled and waved. They were like two mice blindly climbing and scurrying around in their cell. But they had been caught in my trap.

Later after falling in for my shift I found out I would not be in a squad car that night but would be walking beats 4 through 6. The Captain instructed me to be on the look out for some one that had been taking news paper stands and smashing them on the grown to obtain the coins in the coin box. I was taken by the paddy wagon and dropped off in the area and began to walk my beat. Later in the evening just before dark I was walking through the back alley of the local stores and suddenly heard a loud banging noise coming from the alley. As I neared the location of where the noise was coming from there stood a young boy with the news stand trying to smash the coin holder off. When he saw me he took off running. He was fast and there was no way for me to outrun him. The alley was a few blocks long and there was another alley that broke off and circled around and came back into the main alley. I had walked this alley many times checking the doors on the rear of the business places. Well the mouse was outrunning me but then he made an error of judgment. I have always wondered why he scurried into the alley that circled around back into the main alley but it really did not matter with the exception that when I saw him running into that alley I continued to run down to where it returned back into the main alley where I was. Yes there he was running toward me looking back when all of a sudden I tackled him and got my handcuffs on him. Apparently he was not familiar with that side alley. I was because I had tried to cut through there before. Well he had fallen into the trap that I had to set very quickly. His arrest halted the breaking into newspaper stands and when I took him to book him at the Police station I noticed my other two mice were no longer climbing all over the cell. I asked about them and was told that the Juvenile authorities had picked them up. I looked at the booking clerk and told him well here is another one for them to pick up. I guess that makes three. Oh did I misspell mice?

Crossbar Motel

As I have mentioned there were many events that were laughable as I served on the Pensacola Police Force. Once while I was patrolling in the southern part of the downtown area I made a left turn near the old courthouse and lo and behold I saw a woman walking in the middle of the street. I noticed that she was staggering quite a bit. All of a sudden she saw my car and waved her arms back and forth calling out Taxi, Taxi, Taxi. I pulled up beside her and she opened the back door and jumped in the back seat. She looked at me and said I need to find a hotel. I said ok and drove toward the Police station where we had our city jail. She continued to talk a lot until suddenly she looked at my uniform and the metal screen that divided the front seats from the rear. Say what is this she asked, this is not a taxi. I said sure it is but we only have one motel we take people to. It's called the crossbar Motel.

I finally arrived at the station and parked in the rear of the building where the paddy wagon was that had just brought other prisoners in. When I took the intoxicated female into the station the desk Sergeant looked at her and said we just released her a couple of hours ago. She must have headed straight to the bar.

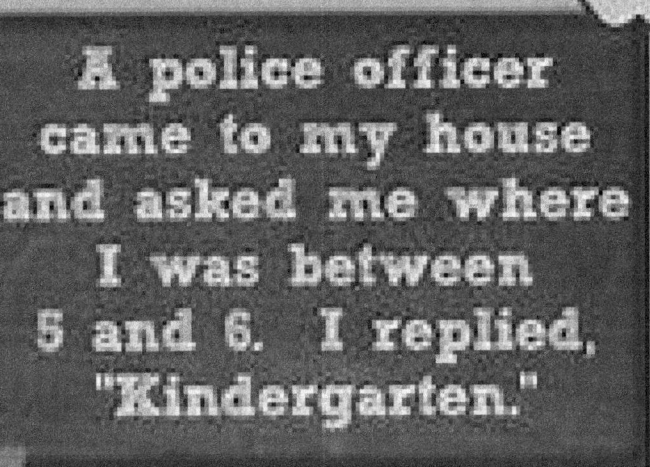

A police officer came to my house and asked me where I was between 5 and 6. I replied, "Kindergarten."

Unique Teaching Resources

Army vehicle disappears

AN Australian Army vehicle worth $74,000 has gone missing after being painted with camouflage.

Police are seeking public help to find the four-wheel drive, which was

Capture of the Prison Escapees

Some months later while patrolling the central section of downtown Pensacola in car 19, I suddenly heard the call come over the radio, "Attention all cars we have received a report that a car with some escaped convicts from Raiford prison are reported coming across the Pensacola Bridge from Gulf Breeze, Florida". Instantly, the radio was filled with several cars responding and the patrol officers saying they were in the vicinity. As I was in the downtown area and quite a distance from where they had given the location I did not respond but continued to listen as a description of the convict's vehicle was given. It seemed like only a few minutes later that I heard radio reports of a chase in progress. Apparently, one of the Patrol cars had spotted their car on east Gregory Street and began pursuit which turned into a high-speed chase. I heard another Patrol car state that they were also behind the getaway car and were in pursuit. As they gave their locations, I could hear their sirens screaming and knew they were headed toward me. Here I was in downtown Pensacola patrolling on Garden Street and quickly made up my mind that they would be headed toward me at any moment. Suddenly there they were making a turn heading north onto Palafox street. With tires squealing, red light flashing, and siren blowing I joined the chase. I was the last of the patrol cars that had joined in the chase and there were two patrol cars in front of me. Suddenly they made a right turn onto Baylen Street heading east. During the high-speed chase, it appeared that the patrol cars were almost on their tail when the escapees started making turns right on Palafox, then right on the next street right again. I began to consider the possibility that if I turned right on Railroad Street and went back to Garden Street I could intercept them on Garden Street. So as all the other patrol cars continued behind them, when I got to Railroad Street I turned right and got back onto Garden Street. I was correct and when they saw me blocking their way they turned right onto a dirt road that ran beside a rail track. The rails were very high and their tires could not jump them at the speed and angle they were traveling. When they noted that the tracks dead-ended and there was no way out they stopped. I had been in hot pursuit and followed them down the dirt road until their vehicle came to a halt. They jumped out of the car leaving the doors wide open and began to run. I jumped out with my gun in hand and began to chase them firing a shot over their head. It only took the one shot and they stopped in their tracks with their hands raised and I was able to subdue them and place my handcuffs on them. They still seemed to be in shock that they had been captured. Our Captain who had now arrived on the scene was very happy with the way that I had preplanned the direction that the escapees would travel and that I was able to apprehend these criminals who had escaped from the state prison in Central Florida.

Weeks after the capture I received a reward of $100.00 for my part in the capture which I shared with a motorcycle officer that got his Motorcycle tangled up in the railroad track while he was trying to help me head them off. Later when we searched the car we found a lot of contraband and a weapon which I am glad that they had decided to abandon when the jumped out of the car. It could have been so easy for the escapees to have had a shootout between us. But that is the danger one suffers when one is just a Cop.

Pensacola at the turn of the 20th Century

Courtesy of Lt Steve Ramos

Jewelry Store Heist

One thing about the possibility of being shot or killed in the line of duty is normally, that there is no warning. Also, it is afterward that you realize how close you came to the Grim Reaper.

At around 11:15 p.m. after being located on my beat for foot patrol in the downtown business area of West Pensacola, I casually began to make my way into the alley's and the back of the business's to check the doors to make sure none had been left unlocked or had been broken into. This beat is quite a distance away from the downtown area, so instead of riding in the paddy wagon with the other foot Patrolmen; I was dropped off by one of the squad cars working that area. As I departed the car I traveled around making the routine checks which were required. After making these checks, I walked back to the main Street of Cervantes where I spotted a red convertible parked with a white male in the car with the top down. He was just sitting in the red convertible with the motor running casually smoking a cigarette. Not thinking anything was amiss, I walked by to check out the remainder of the business area,

He smiled at me as I passed his car. Now as you read this, one would naturally wonder why I was not worried about his presence at this hour of the night. Why would this person be just sitting out in front of one of the businesses with the motor running? Well the reason it did not worry me was the fact that upstairs was the Conger Insurance Company, where agents many times were known to work late pulling their accounts so I just assumed that he was waiting for one of the other agents to come down. Later I returned and passed by the Convertible which was still there with the motor running, and walked up the stairs, where the entrance door to the offices were, including the Conger Insurance Company which was in one of the offices inside. Walking past the doorway into the hallway I made my way toward the office, making a right turn then a left turn I looked ahead at the door for the Conger Insurance Company and took hold of the door knob and noted it was locked and there were no lights on in the inside. Almost at the same instance that I realized no one was in the Insurance office, suddenly I heard footsteps running down the stairwell I had just climbed. Immediately I turned around and ran back down the hallway toward the exit almost crashing into the open door which had been closed earlier just inside the hallway but now was open. I was not aware at the time but just moments earlier when I passed that door two burglars were hiding inside, holding a shotgun waiting for me to come into the room where they were.

They were hidden behind the then closed door of an empty room just inside the hall entrance. Quickly I looked inside the room, and lo and behold to my utter amazement I spotted where the flooring had been torn away. There before me was a large hole for entrance into the room below. It did not take but a moment for me to realize that I was seeing a crime scene. As I ran down the stairs I heard the squeal of tires as the red convertible raced off into the night. With my gun in my hand, I screamed halt, but they were too far away for me to fire, and I watched as the red convertible disappeared in the distance. It was then that I turned around and saw that I was standing in front of the local Jewelry store. Lifting my eyes and gazing upstairs I noted this business was below the room where they had been tearing out the floor, I had just stopped an actual burglary in progress. They had been tearing out the flooring above to gain entrance into the Jewelry store

Running down the street to the corner I opened the call box and reported the burglary. I gave the description of the car and soon a patrol car arrived on the scene and they took over the crime scene. It was surprising how close they had been to completing the tearing away of the floor. When I was asked to describe the driver of the convertible I told the Investigator that he looked similar to "Jimmy" who ran the news stand on Palafox Street in downtown Pensacola but I quickly added, "It was not Jimmy".

The following night when we were about to leave the station, I described the getaway driver to the officer that walked the beat downtown. As I described the description of the car and the driver, he quickly replied, "That's Sonny Roche, Cocky Roche's son. I see him every night driving downtown to the nightclub Trader John's." Well, the next time you see him pick him up for me and I will come in and sign the warrant I instructed.

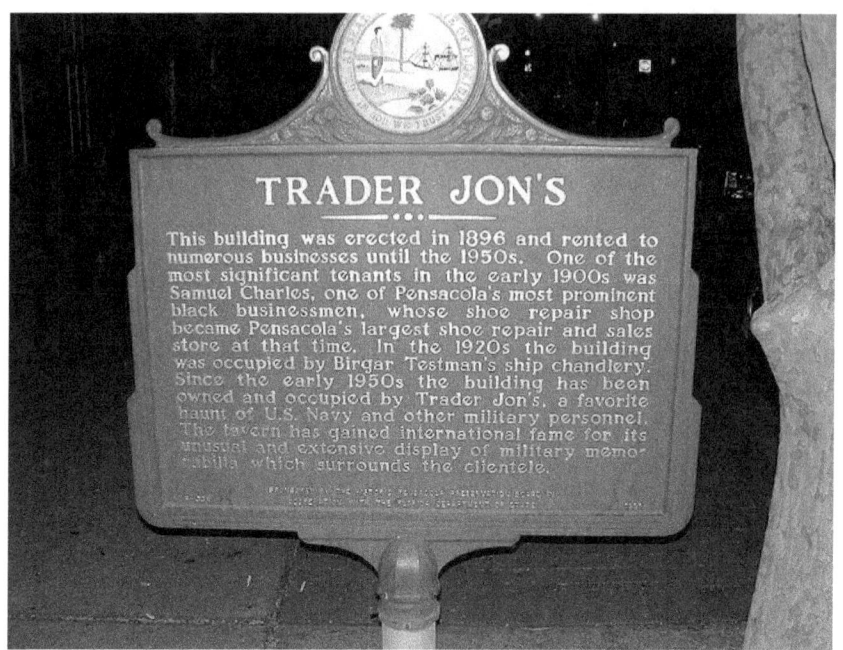

The following night he informed me that he had picked up Cocky Roche's son but the shift Captain had let him go saying "Oh Cocky Roche's son would never do that! Later I discovered that the Captain was his uncle. End of story? No, I called the County Sheriff, Bill Davis and explained what had occurred. They put a tail on the son and a week later caught the gang robbing another jewelry store. It was after the capture of the gang that I found out how fortunate I was because I was told that they were ready to blow me apart if I had entered the room where they were waiting behind the closed door.

As a result of the capture of this gang burglary in the area decreased for some time.

Many years later I learned that this gang had always performed their acts of burglary when a certain watch captain was on duty and that the operation had stemmed over into my watch because of the problem they had getting through the floor of the Jewelry store. There was no investigation that I know of to expose that Captain and some years later he retired. When speaking with my fellow officer Joseph who had done his job well in taking Roche in he related how that Roche and the others got together on many occasions at Trader Johns. Trader Johns was a very popular joint with many Navy personal in my days on the force as well as many civilians. As you might have noted there is a plaque that displays the memory of Trader Johns.

A cop is staking out a bar for drunk drivers. At closing time, he sees a guy stumble out of the bar, trip on the curb, and fumble for his keys for five minutes. When he finally gets in, it takes him another five minutes to get the key in the ignition. Meanwhile, everybody else leaves the bar and drives off. When he finally pulls away, the cop is waiting for him, pulls him over, and gives him a Breathalyzer test. The test shows he has a blood alcohol level of 0.0. The cop says, 'How is this possible?' The guy says, 'Tonight I'm the designated decoy.'

A cop pulls over a guy. "Your eyes are awfully red. Have you been drinking?" "Gee, officer," the man ays. "Your eyes are awfully glazed ave you been eating doughnuts?".

The Girl with the Red hair

On another night while patrolling on West Cervantes Street I noticed a white female with red hair standing next to the street and I noted that when she spotted my patrol car, she hastily retreated walking down the sidewalk. Looking around to see if I had spotted her she smiled a big smile as I drove up. I began to question her because we had had reports of hookers working in the Brownsville area. I asked her what had she been doing and she replied, "oh I am on my way to the store. Why? What's up officer?" Could you show me some I.D.? I asked? She did not have any, so I asked her what her name was. With a big grin, she stared me in the eyes and said oh my name is Joyce Taylor, what's your name Officer? Officer Duke, I answered. I then asked her what she did for a living. Smiling again and looking into my eyes she said, Oh I seem to be without a job at the moment. Where do you live I asked? Well, I actually do not have anywhere at the moment as I lost my room with some friends. I then said Joyce I am going to have to arrest you for Vagrancy and Loitering. Why would you do that Duke? Because we have had complaints that women have been working the street here in Brownsville selling sexual favors and we have been asked to clear the street of anyone that did not have a job and was on the street loitering especially if they had no I.D. or place to live. On the way to the jail at the Police Station Joyce kept smiling at me and chatting. Finally, I got her booked, fingerprinted, and left her at the jail where she got a bunk and two meals a day until she was released.

The next day one of the Policemen that had worked at the jail teased me about my violent offender I had arrested who wrote my name all over the walls of the jail cell with love symbols. What in the world did you do to her, he asked? I arrested her and that's all, was my reply. But she did chat her head off all the way to the Police Station I added.

Later that night I received a call that there had been a burglary at a general store off West Garden Street. After finding the building, I left my car parked and began to walk around in the dark streets nearby. All of a sudden I saw a black male and called for him to halt. Well he did not halt but took off running. I fired over his head and that was the last I saw of him. My problem after this was that I had to write a report on, why I had fired my weapon and turn it in to the Chief of Police. Later I thought about that suspect and what might have caused him to disappear so quickly.

Smoky the Crooked Cop

Many of the Police Officers I worked with during my time on the force were great Cops. But as in any workplace there are always some that are on the shady side. When you work close to them in a squad car for eight hours the true person is usually revealed. Many of them have traits that range from vulgar to cruelty. As I pointed out earlier I wanted to be a good Cop and attempted to treat others as I would want to be treated. I was twinned up one night with a man that was popular on the force because of his many talents.

He had a great singing voice and was respected by the department for his ability to handle life and death situations. Smoky Peaden opened the door of the squad car that night that I rode together with him in a two manned Patrol car. Almost instantly as he slowly settled in his seat he began to use vulgar language. Was this the same man that I had heard so much about? My understanding was that he sang in the Police and gospel group and was a Christian.

The remainder of my shift I was appalled at all of the foul words that was in is vocabulary. I was so glad when the shift ended that night and I could get away. As I was working on the D squad and Smoky now had been assigned to our squad I began to see him every night at role call. Almost every time I ran into him he had to use profanity.

I received quite a shock one day when I was driving my car from my home to a car lot in Warrington. I turned my radio on and lo and behold I recognized the voice of the disc jockey. I checked to see if I had tuned in the gospel station and yes it was on the gospel station. I listened again to make sure that the voice I was hearing was the one I thought it was when all of a sudden he gave his name. This is your gospel buddy Smoky Peaden coming to you today. Yes I was correct with that voice, but what, how, why is he on the gospel station? Later after many weeks had passed I found out that Smoky was running for Political office in the state.

During this time my brother Bob Duke was working with the Pensacola News Journal Newspaper and I noticed that Bob had begun to back him. Surprised by this I decided to say nothing, but later I found out that Bob had backed off with his support. It was then that I spoke to Bob again and this time I related to him all that I knew about Smoky Peaden. Well Smoky was elected to the Florida House of Representatives (representing District 2) in 1972 and re-elected in 1974. My thoughts were always on I wonder how long he will last in office. During his tenure in office the Escambia High School riots broke out, and the events leading up to them took place. Peaden and fellow legislator W. D. Childers voiced sympathy for white students and parents and offered to explain the "seriousness of the white backlash" to the NAACP but apparently to no avail because on February 25, 1976, Peaden's home was destroyed by an arsonist. Peaden was allegedly planning a 1980 run for the office of Escambia County Sheriff when he was brought up on several drug charges. Witnesses claimed Peaden had trafficked cocaine with the intent to use the profits to fund his political campaign. Peaden denied distributing drugs and testified that he approached the State Attorney Curtis Golden in 1979 to provide names of drug dealers.

He was convicted on five counts on August 18, 1982, which was affirmed on appeal. Well my hunch was correct. You can always know a person by their actions. It has always been my belief that most politicians use religion as a tool to gain votes but after they are in office then you really get to know them by their deeds. Those that are close to an individual normally know them for what they really are.

Cops on the Prowl

Later after making that raid we traveled to another address which also was being used as a house of ill repute. This time I waited on the outside with some of the others that was in on the raid. I walked around to one side of the house and spotted a figure looking out of a bedroom window then slowly climbing outside. As I studied him still standing near the window I noted it was one of our police officers. As I watched him I thought to myself, I do not remember him being on our watch tonight. Oh well maybe he was a undercover cop so I was not bothered about it. Well I did find out later that when the Captain walked in on him he was under the cover! Later he walked over to me and said Duke the Captain let me slip out after he realized who I was and that I was with one of the girls. So make sure you do not tell anyone that you saw me. Then he took off walking as fast as he could. Later I asked the Captain about the situation and he laughed and said, Yes, I let him go. I have never seen anyone as scared as him when we walked into his room and found him in bed with that girl. I thought he was going to have a heart attack. Later I heard through the grapevine that the Captain had known in advance that there were some Police Officers at this particular place of ill repute. I could never find out who the other ones were as the Captain failed to share his secret with us. Had I found out who they were I might have been able to find out the real reason for the raid. But it was late and my shift was ending and I wanted to go home for some R&R.

Oh No Not the Red headed Girl again

The house is no longer there. It was
located on Baylen Street and anyone
passing by would never have suspected
what it was being used for with the
exception of the women that worked there
and the men that frequented it. I had
personally passed the house many times
because of its location but never
suspected that it was being used as a
cathouse. But sooner or later they would
find out that Crime does not pay and that
was one Saturday night on the midnight
shift. As we fell on to formation the shift

Captain informed us that we would be making a raid on a Cathouse that night. Most of us had never been on a raid before so we were a little excited about one of the officers on the hit. Around one AM we all gathered nearby and surrounded the house. The Captain then asked me to go in with him while the other cops kept the house surrounded. As we walked into the front room a woman met us and screamed out Oh No! The Captain told her to be quite and to have all of the guests and girls to come into the front room. As I looked toward the door it opened and guess who I spotted? She was one of the first girls to exit the bedroom area. Yes there she was, the red headed girl that I had arrested in Brownsville. When she saw me she smiled a big smile and said Well hello Duke we meet again. I always wondered if I would see you again Duke. Well for the second time I had to give her room and accommodation again at the crossbar Motel. I was shocked when the Captain had us to arrest the girls but allowed their clients to go free. Later I asked him why the others were not arrested and was told that the reason for the girls to be arrested was to insure that they received sexual disease examinations and was clean. The next morning in court they received a fine but they also had to spend time in jail waiting until they had tests to determine if they were free from sexual disease. Did she write my name all over the cell again? Well no reports that she did unless it was hidden where no one could see it. Also I found out later that all the girls had tested negative and had been released as soon as the results had come in. I have always wondered if Joyce remained in the trade as I never had any news that she had been arrested again. Maybe she had learned her lesson or maybe she had found one of those cops that we had caught in the other houses of ill repute to marry. Well you and I will never know will we?

Medina

Police went to a North State Street address just after midnight Nov. 20 after getting a call about a disturbance. Officers found an engaged couple there arguing about what time Kmart closed. Police told them the store's hours and the couple calmed down.

Doctor on the prowl

Oh my, look at him go? He must be in a hurry? He's traveling way over the speed limit. I quickly made a u-turn and sped after him. As I turned my red light on and sounded my siren I noticed that he was trying to speed up even faster. But I was in one of the new Dodge patrol cars that we had just received, and oh was it fast. Before long I had pulled up behind him and he slowed pulling his car over to the side. I reached over for my ticket book, stepped out of my cruiser slowly walked up beside the vehicle I had pulled over for speeding. Well it is not often that a Cop stops a speeding vehicle and when he walks up to the vehicle there is his Physician sitting behind the wheel. As I looked inside, I was surprised to see my personal Doctor behind the wheel. I said Doctor, where are you headed? He looked at me and spoke in a nervous voice; Oh I am headed for the hospital was his reply. I have an emergency there that I have to attend, that's why I am speeding. Ok Doctor which Hospital. Baptist, he replied. I said ok follow me but I quickly noted he was traveling in the wrong direction to get to the Baptist Hospital.

Oh, you do not have to escort me, he said. Doctor just follow me I will get you there just keep close behind me. I jumped back in the car and with my red light flashing and my siren blowing; I escorted the Doctor to the Baptist Hospital. Later after doing a little checking, I found out the Doctor had a girlfriend that he was late going to meet. Hmmm, I wonder if she was still there when he finally arrived. Could she have been the red headed girl now at the cross bar Motel? Well I will never know.

I was surprised years later to find out that this Doctor who we loved so much because of his birthing our children and performing surgery on me eventually ended up having a alcohol problem and finally gave up the profession. Even in spite of his weakness's he will always be remembered as a fine Doctor that did not over charge his patients but treated his patients with love and kindness.

T.T. Wentworth Museum

My two Resisting Arrest

We had been walking our assigned beat and had made our area check when I came to the corner of my beat and Officer Joseph who was on the next beat walked up and said, let's go get some coffee. Talking about what we had been doing and the cold freezing weather we headed to the only coffee place nearby. It was freezing and the wind was blowing quite a bit as we walked into the Greyhound Bus Terminal to get a cup. As we walked up to the counter of the Cafeteria the cashier pointed out a man slumped over in one of the seats and asked us to do something with him. We walked over to where the man was slumped over and we attempted to awaken him but to no avail. Finally, Officer Joseph got under one arm and I under the other to move him outside to be picked up by the paddy wagon. As we carried him outside, all of a sudden he felt the freezing rain and wind and came alive, fighting and kicking screaming, "Let me go", using all types of foul language. Well, I kept my hold on him trying to keep him subdued never thinking of using my billy club on him. But Officer Joseph had other ideas. He pulled out his slapjack and hit the man and then lost control of his slapjack. It fell on the sidewalk and he let the man go and left me to wrestle with the drunk alone. The man went wild punching at me so finally, I pulled out my slap jack and hit him on the side of his head. Instantly he stopped fighting with me, sat down on the pavement and started crying out holding his head. Well, the paddy wagon arrived and we put him inside to be taken for treatment for his injury and then to be booked at the City Jail located behind the City police station.

The next day I had to appear in court to testify against him. I felt so sorrowful when I saw where I had hit him in the head. When I testified I told the Judge that he did not know what he was doing, all he knew was two men were hauling him outdoors and he resisted. Well, the Judge found him guilty of being drunk in a public place and resisting arrest. This was one of only two resisting arrests during my many years with the Pensacola Police Department in Pensacola, Florida. The other offense was when I arrested a young male in the local downtown Theatre. This was on a Saturday night at the Midnight show. I was called to take him out of the theatre and when we got outside he started fighting with me and attempted to return to the theatre. Finally, to protect myself I pulled my club and hit him once which caused him to come under submission.

. Over the years I wrote a lot of tickets, some when I was walking a beat and others when I was on car patrol. I also investigated a lot of wrecks and was involved in many arrests in which all but one was found guilty of the charges that they committed. During the time that I served on the Pensacola Police Department, I was happy with my fellow workers because we all tried to look after each other. If we would have had a slogan, it would have been the one used by Robin Hood, One for all and all for one, I can not remember any time that I had a problem with my fellow officers. Normally in any work or job place, most of the fellow workers are there to do a job well and are honest in their work. I would venture to say 90% of my fellow Police Officers were there because they wanted to do a good job and do it right, but there are always the few in any type of job that are trouble but normally we know them by their works..

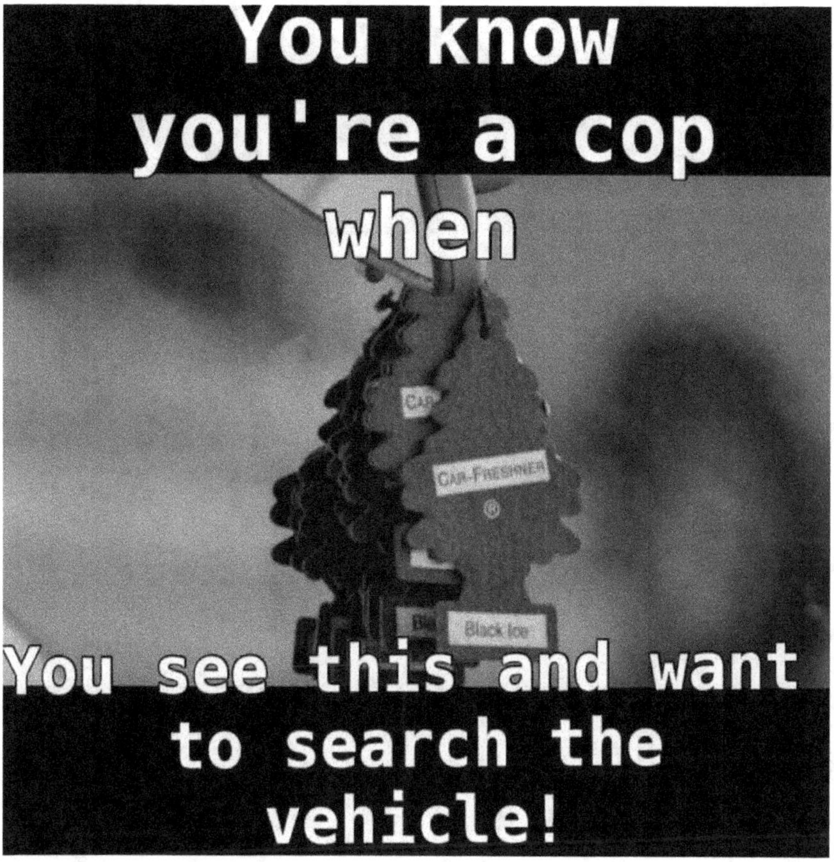

You know you're a cop when

You see this and want to search the vehicle!

WHERE IS THE TOILET PAPER?

I heard a call come in on the radio that there was a situation on the corner of Maxwell Street and 10th Avenue but because I was on another call the dispatcher assigned it to another unit. As I was not assigned the call and we continued to be very busy during the remainder of that shift which was the three to eleven I let the call fade from my thoughts even though it was a location near my residence. Later when I got off duty and went home guess what I saw in front of my house and on my house. Yes it was toilet paper all over the trees, yard, and house. They did miss the garage where I parked my car. As I slowly got out of the car and look around at all the toilet paper every where Carol came out and told me that she had called the incident in and they had sent a policeman out who took a report on the occurrence. I then asked her if she had seen who had been responsible for this act. Her answer was no but she said I called up Pastor Glass and told him what had happened and asked him if I should take further action. Well when he answered the phone and I told him all he could do was laugh. Then he related to me how that the very same thing had happened to his home. I asked him if he had ever found out who did it and he started laughing again. Finally he said Sister Duke I can guess who the culprits were and if you would let me handle it I will make them come back out and remove it. Later we learned through the grape vine that it had been some of the youth from the church that had done it for a joke. Well we laughed and took no further action.

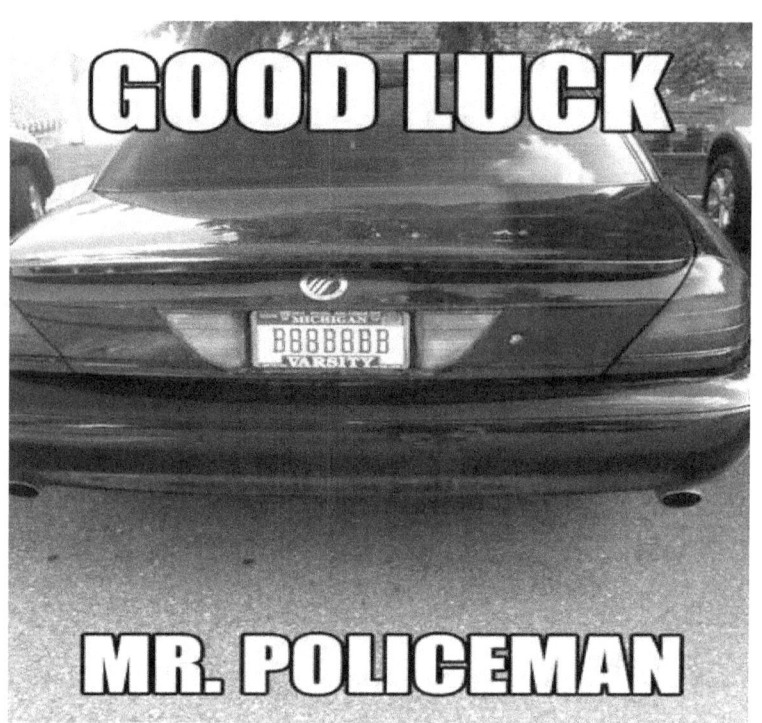

SORRY NOT LOOKING

I was on my way to the Police station which was about a block from Garden Street. As I slowed down and stopped at the red light I watched the light change to green then began to make a right turn on 9th Avenue. All of a sudden I heard tires squealing and then a bang. As I was already leaving the scene I continued on until I could pull over and then looked around to see what had occurred. I saw where two cars had collided and there was a patrol car pulling in behind them. Well I will let them handle this accident. Later the officer that did the report related that he had to investigate an accident where one of the drivers had taken her eyes off the road because she had seen a Policeman in front of her and was rushing to see if it was one that she knew. I asked him what her name was and he said Choy. I begin to think about that last name for a minute and then I asked was her first name Martha. He said yes how did you know? I then told him that I had to go to her residence on a prowler call. I checked the area out but could not find any signs of a prowler. After letting her know what I had found out she wanted me to come in and have coffee. As I was on duty and had calls coming I told her that I would have to refrain because I had other calls. After leaving she begins to make calls that suspicious people were around her home and would ask the dispatcher to send me. Later I noticed that her car would be near my residence when I got home. Sometimes I would hear a car circling the block and would look out and see her car. Then all of a sudden it stopped.

The AAA Scandal

I had not been on the force long and found out that there were ways to make a little extra money if you were involved in investigating an accident. One of my fellow officers informed me that there were Automobile wrecker companies that would pay you twenty-five dollars if you called them to an accident scene and they were able to pick up one of the vehicles involved in the accident. When I was told this I thought wow that will be great and I looked forward to being able to work my first accident. I soon found out that the only cops that made this money were the ones doing traffic patrol which was handled by the Motorcycle or squad car Patrolmen. Of course, there was that hope that one day after I had been there and worked up to this type of duty I would be able to achieve these rewards. Well, the desire was soon squashed one day when the Pensacola News Journal's Morning newspaper screamed with the headlines AAA claims Pensacola Police were taking bribes and called it a wrecker payola scheme. That day when I went to work the Police department was abuzz with the news and who might be indicted for accepting bribes. The problem arose over some of the Police officers investigating the wreck and when a victim in the accident requested a particular towing company the Officer would tell them that that company was not on the approved Wrecker list and would recommend another company that he knew would pay the fee. When I found out what was happening I knew that this had been the wrong thing to do. One by one the investigators sifted through the evidence given by the AAA and one by one we had Patrolman and Officers to resign. I remember one of the Captains that owned a gas station that I purchased my gas from would run out and keep asking me what was going on at the station. He was always nervous as he asked about the situation. I later found out that he was one of the ones involved and that he had resigned from the force and was worried that he might also be charged with a criminal act. The worst part of all of this was the bad name that the department received as that hurt the image of all the Policemen that were not involved.

Other than this situation I was very proud of the Pensacola Police Department for their stand on equality. We were instructed to treat everyone in the same manner when issuing tickets even if they were a local official.

Jim Joins the Force

Before becoming a Police Officer I had a
turn at trying to sell life and hospital
insurance. I had worked at it for about 4
months and found that it was not my line
of work. During the time though, I came
in contact with Jim Billy Barnes who
became a great friend of mine. It's strange
how you come into contact with many
people from different phases of life then
there comes one that you seem to get on
with more so than others and you begin to
count them as your friend,

After I had been on the Police force for a
number of years and trying to get Jim to

join he suddenly decided he would try his hand at becoming a policeman. Well, he was accepted and was sent to the Police Academy where all Policemen have to be trained. After his graduation from the Academy I don't know how it happened, but when he came to work on the force he ended up on my shift and I was asked to train him. Further training consisted of his riding with an experienced officer for several weeks in a squad car then being placed on the walking beat till his seniority placed him back in a patrol car. Well, the first night that we were on the midnight shift we began to patrol the downtown area. Around 2:00 am after the streets had died down and the bars had closed we began checking alleys behind some of the downtown businesses. There was one long alley behind the major shops that you entered and drove a block and it turned right then the alley came to a dead end. When I entered the alley I noticed Jim was napping and when I made the right turn there in the alley was a pack of dogs snarling and tearing into the garbage cans. I stuck my arm out the window, sped up the car, and began beating against the car as loud as I could scream, there they are let's get them. Jim Billy sprung up almost scared to death. Well, I laughed afterward but he did not find it very funny. Jim did well on the Police force and stayed on even after I left and eventually rose to be a Police Captain. Years later the PPD held a commemoration for him when he passed away.

Later Jim and I traveled over to Cagle's Restaurant for a cup of coffee. As I walked in, I noticed Pastor Glass sitting at one of the tables. When he saw me he made a statement I will never forget. Duke you are a big man but I know someone that is bigger than you! Years later I would find that Great big God. You can read all about my turning to Christ in my book Guns to the Gospel.

A Real Miracle

One Saturday night after I had begun to go to church and live for the Lord I was cruising down West Cervantes street on patrol duty and as I approached the lights at A Street, a car stopped for the red signal on A Street suddenly ran the red light. It was a small MG and I immediately began a pursuit after him. Thoughts began to rush through my mind as to why he had run the light. My conclusion was, he must be wanted for some criminal offense and when he saw me he took off. As I began to pursue him he began to hit high speeds of 80-100

MPH The chase at high speeds and fast turns eventually led us to Cervantes and A Street, His small Mg would pull away from me on the turns but in the high-speed dodge I was driving I would gain on him on the straight run. E Street was downhill and as I started to gain on him again doing around 80 mph suddenly at the bottom of the hill he made a left turn. I also started making the turn and suddenly I lost control of the car, When my car lost control I remember closing my eyes and throwing my hand up in the air and cried out to the Lord, Jesus help me. All I heard was squealing of tires and the rear end of my car swinging around. When I cried out to the Lord all of a sudden the car straightened up, I opened my eyes and to my surprise, I was still in the pursuit. One block away he tried to make another turn but the sand in the road caused him to lose control and he hit a fence and ended up in the yard of a homeowner.

I got out of the car with my weapon drawn and had him to allow me to cuff him. I then asked him why in the world were you running from me. His reply was I ran the red light then saw you after me. On further criminal checks indeed that was all he had done.

The next day after this incident I traveled back to the scene to see what caused my car to lose control then suddenly it straightened out. I parked my car and went over to the corner and as I studied the curb I saw black tire marks all over the curb. Apparently the curb was very high above the street on that corner and as the rear end of my vehicle as it twisted around it hit the curb and that stopped my vehicles loss of control. I have always believed that God had his hand upon me at this time because I know beyond a shadow of doubt that I could have ended up dead or in the hospital. Yes I had been saved from another near death incident.

114

CAPTURE OF THE MAD THUG

It was really a dark night that I received a call that there was a wanted person that had been spotted at a West Pensacola address. Several of other Policemen responded to the call as well as me. When we arrived and parked about a block away plans were made on how we would force him out of the home that he had entered. Each one of us were assigned a area in order to surround the building on all sides in order to prevent him from escaping. After deciding where each man would be we went back to our cars and gathered our weapons that we would be using in the arrest. I reached inside my car and pulled out my automatic shotgun which I had only had to use once before in a foiled robbery on the south end of West Pensacola. As I picked up my weapon and walked to my assigned area I noted that the other Cops had reached their positions and as they knelt down the Captain took up a loud speaker and began to speak demanding that the man come out and give himself up. Nothing happened so the Captain spoke again demanding that he come out and surrender or we were going to break the door down and come in. We waited for about 5 minutes or so and then the Captain instructed 3 officers to go in and get the man out. He looked around and ordered us to hold our positions and make sure to be on the alert in the event that he leaves the house and attempts to escape. There holding my shotgun ready for anything that might happen I stood and then all of a sudden he came running out toward me. I held my shotgun on him and he stopped. All of a sudden he had cops all over him and after he was handcuffed they picked him up and as he passed me he stared me right in the eye and said you think you are a big man with that shotgun in your hand don't you? I just returned his stare and did not answer.

Later in the evening I received another call just south of the location where we had captured the wanted person. Shots had been fired and I turned on my red light and peeled off as fast as I could travel toward the address where another fellow officer might be in trouble. I arrived to find that the area had been surrounded and I took up my assigned position. Then I heard more shots coming from the inside of the house. The Captain spoke on the horn and ordered the man to lay down his weapon. The man responded by firing another shot. It appeared that there was only one way to get that man out so we considering using tear gas but at the time we had none so we devised another plan. One officer would get to the rear of the house and look for a way to slip inside. A few officers would draw his attention to the front of the house and when they did the officer would slip in from the rear and capture him. So we drew his attention first by talking to him and asking him to give himself up. As he responded to our request and let us know that No I am not surrendering nor laying my gun down, officer Mandel my old mate slipped through a back window he had found unlocked and silent slipped up behind the perpetrator and placed his gun in his back and let him know you make a move I am going to shoot you. The man instantly dropped his weapon and threw up his hands and began to cry please don't shoot me Please don't shoot me. After handcuffing him we found out that this entire dilemma had escalated from a domestic dispute. Over the years I discovered that domestic disputes were the most dangerous call a cop had to handle. Many Police Officers have been killed in the handling of a family argument. Law Enforcement Officers are being murdered as well as laying down their lives on duty every 58 hours. They are being shot while sitting at traffic lights. Executed in coffee shops and on their lunch breaks. Lured into ambushes and blown away while removing debris from the roadway, or while responding to an alarm call which was a set up. They are being killed in their own driveways, while off duty. They are being shot inside their own precincts. If celebrities or professional athletes were being targeted, shot and murdered to the tune of one dead every 58 hours there would be an instant demand for answers and protection. There would be a national cry to stop the violence before it impacted reality TV or sports center. Regardless of proven statistics which tell us otherwise, our officers continue to get blamed as a whole for the actions of less than one percent*. Regardless of common sense in a world where we have all encountered a bad mechanic, doctor, plumber, we blame ALL cops for the few. Regardless of countless corrupt priests, teachers, crooked judges and lawyers, we do not condemn their entire profession, it's asinine to even consider. But with law enforcement, it is instant condemnation of all. I would like to leave you with the following advice and hope it might be of use.

What NOT to say to a Police Officer

- I can't reach my licence unless you hold my beer.
- Is that a 9mm? That's nothing look at my 44 Magnum.
- You must have been going over 120 to keep up with me.
- Sorry Officer my radar detector wasn't plugged in.
- I was going to be a cop but I decided to finish high school instead.
- Are you the guy from the Village People?
- Bad Cop. No donut.
- Your not going to check my truck are you?
- Gee that gut doesn't inspire confidence.
- Didn't I see you get your butt kicked on Cops?
- I pay your salary.
- Wow, you look like the guy in the picture on my girlfriends night stand.
- I thought you had to be in good shape to be a police officer.
- Is it true people become cops because they can't get a job at McDonalds?
- Well, when I reached down to pick up my bag of crack, my gun fell out and lodged between the brake and gas

omg she blocked me..!

PLEASE TAKE ME TO JAIL

One Monday I received a call telling me to investigate a breaking and entering at the Waterfront Mission. I was quite a distance away and turned on my red light but no siren. On the TV I notice that most of the time Hollywood enjoys having the police car in the middle of the night to travel with the siren screaming and blue lights flashing. When a Cop actually goes to a scene where the culprits might still be in the building or the vicinity they normally do not use the siren as it warns them off. I finally reached the Mission and was taken into the kitchen where the dastardly deed had been committed. The burglar had forced open the food freezer which had a lock. The lock had been broken and there before me were the remains of the food he left behind.

Apparently he must have been interrupted in his theft because I also saw where he had eaten some food and left the empty wrappings. He also must have taken food With him more than likely what he could carry in his pockets hidden away. Well I took all the information down and checked out the inside of the building in order to be sure the thief was not still there. After checking the building I then began to drive around the area and yes I found him. He was still having a snack. He did not attempt to run but just sat there eating away. I asked him where he had gotten the food. He did not try to lie but readily told me he got it from the Mission. I said so you stole it? He replied No I was starving and I just borrowed it. Then he made a funny request. Duke please arrest me and take me to jail. I am able to eat there but if you gave me money to buy food I would as hungry as I am still use it to purchase alcohol. Please take me to Jail. So I arrested him for theft and took him to jail.

"Just a Cop Poem"

The funeral line was long,
There's an awful lot of cars,
Folks came out of the restaurants,
They came out of the bars.
The workers at the construction sites
All let their hammers drop.
Someone asked. "What is this all for?"
And they said, "Aw, just a cop."
Some chuckled at the passing cars.
Some shed a silent tear
Some people said, "It's stupid.
all these dumb policemen here."
"How come they're not out fighting'
crime?
Or in a doughnut shop?
Sure is a lot of trouble,
For someone who's just a cop."

They blocked the intersections,
They blocked the interstate.
People yelled and cursed,
"Hey, it's going to make me late!"
"This is really ridiculous!"
"They're making' us all stop!"
"It seems they're sure wasting' time,
On someone who's just a cop."
Into the cemetery now,
The slow procession comes,
The Taps are slowly played.
There's loud salutes from guns.
The graveyard workers shake their heads
"This service is a flop."
"There's lots of words wasted,
On someone who's just a cop."
Yeah, just a cop to most folks.
Did his duty every day.
Trying' to protect us,
Till they took his life away.
And when he got to heaven,
St. Peter put him at the top.
An angel asked him, "Who was that?"
And he said, "Aw, just a cop."

WITTY COP SAYINGS

1-"You know, stop lights don't come any redder than the one you just went through."

2-"Relax, the handcuffs are tight because they're new. They'll Stretch after you wear them a while."

3-"If you run, you'll only go to jail tired."

4-"You don't know how fast you were going? I guess that means I can write anything I want to on the ticket, huh?"

5-"Yes, sir, you can talk to the shift supervisor, but I don't think it will help. Oh, did I mention that I'm the shift supervisor?

"6- "Warning! You want a warning? O.K, I'm warning you not to do that again or

I'll give you another ticket."

7-"The answer to this last question will determine whether you are drunk or not. Was Mickey Mouse a cat or a dog?"

8- "Fair? You want me to be fair? Listen, fair is a place where you go to ride on rides, eat cotton candy and corn dogs and step in monkey poop."

9-"Yeah, we have a quota. Two more tickets and my wife get's a toaster oven."

10-"In God we trust; all others we run through NCIC." (National Crime Information Center)

11-"Just how big were those 'two beers' you say you had?"

12-"No sir, we don't have quotas anymore. We used to, but now we're allowed to write as many tickets as we can."

13-"I'm glad to hear that the Chief (of Police) is a personal friend of yours. So you know someone who can post your bail."

George Phillips of Meridian, Mississippi was going up to bed when his wife told him that he'd left the light on in the garden shed, which she could see from the bedroom window. George opened the back door to go turn off the light but saw that there were people in the shed stealing things. He phoned the police, who asked "Is someone in your house?" and he said "No". Then they said that all patrols were busy, and that he should simply lock his door and an officer would be along when available. George said, "Okay," hung up, counted to 30, and phoned the police again. "Hello, I just called you a few seconds ago because there were people in my shed. Well, you don't have to worry about them now cause I've just shot them all." Then he hung up. Within five minutes three police cars, an Armed Response unit, and an ambulance showed up at the Phillips residence and caught the burglars red-handed. One of the Policemen said to George: "I thought you said that you'd shot them!" George said, "I thought you said there was nobody available!" (True Story) I LOVE IT

The End of being Just a Cop

After serving many years on the Police Force I found Christ and began to be involved in the work of God. I had received such a wonderful experience with Jesus Christ that I wanted to share it with others. Within one year of God giving me the new birth he called me into the ministry. As a result of wanting to advance my ministry I left the Police Force but because I wanted to pioneer new churches and would need funds I continued to work in jobs that were relative to the legal profession I have worked as a Court appointed Process Server in the first Judicial Circuit Court State of Florida. My badge number was 008. During the time that I worked as a

Process server I also held a Private Investigators license for some years and would accept jobs that would not discredit my ministry. Since I used much of the offering and Tithes for the ministry taking only what I needed for expenses and housing I found that when I retired I was unable to get by with just what I received from Social Security so today I am still doing part time work as a Process server. While living in Melbourne, Florida I worked in the Brevard County Circuit badge # 571 for several years and recently I have returned to the 1st Judicial Circuit. When I returned I was not allowed to keep my old badge number and now I have badge #670. There are many things that I have come to be thankful for. The main one is Robert Glass telling me about the new birth. Second that I found the new birth and God used me in the Ministry I would like to also close by saying that I am still thankful that one day God allowed me to be Just a Cop.

Salvation Plan

Salvation could be divided into two categories? The first would be with you accepting the Lord Jesus Christ as your personal Saviour being baptized in water in the name of the titles without following the plan that Jesus spoke to Nicodemus about. This first category takes the chance that even though Jesus Christ did not give me the new birth he has still saved you? This plan takes you to the Judgment of God to find out if your plan was enough. The second category assures you of your salvation as long as you continue with him. This is the one spoken by Jesus Christ in St. John chapter 3 and fulfilled in Acts chapter 2. You need to read both of these chapters and understand that all of the early disciples were recipients of this salvation. So my question to you is: Do you want to be saved in the way Jesus spoke of or in the way the modern church tells you. Here is the bible way: 1- Repent 2- Be baptized in the name of Jesus Christ 3-Let God fill you with his Spirit

ABOUT

Today George Duke edits the following sites where you are able to download bible studies and power point messages as well as read daily Christian News articles from around the world

WWW.WCN4U.COM
WWW.ACTCHURCH.COM
WWW.USANEEDSCHURCHSCHOOLS.COM

At the time of publication George and Carol Duke have been married for over 60 years and have been complimented with a certificate commemorating over 50 years in the Ministry.

Carol Duke has published Aunt Dee's Happy Tails and it can be purchased on Amazon or on Kindle as well as my book Guns to the Gospel.